FIRST TIME LEARNING
Writing

For Preschool and Early Years

Illustrated by
Andy Cooke

Designed and produced by
Autumn Publishing Ltd
Chichester, West Sussex, UK

© 2004 Autumn Publishing Ltd

Printed in Spain

ISBN 1 904586 39 2

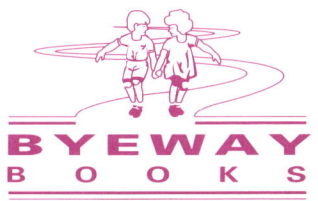

BYEWAY
B O O K S

Straight lines

Lines are everywhere.
How many lines can you see around you?

Can you find a sticker
of a stripy butterfly?

Trace the lines to draw stripes on the snake.
Draw more tall grass.

Trace the lines to draw stripes on the tiger.
Now let's make it rain! Draw rain coming from the clouds
in straight lines.

Well done! Every time you finish a page,
put your reward sticker here.

Down and across

Trace the lines on the roller coaster.

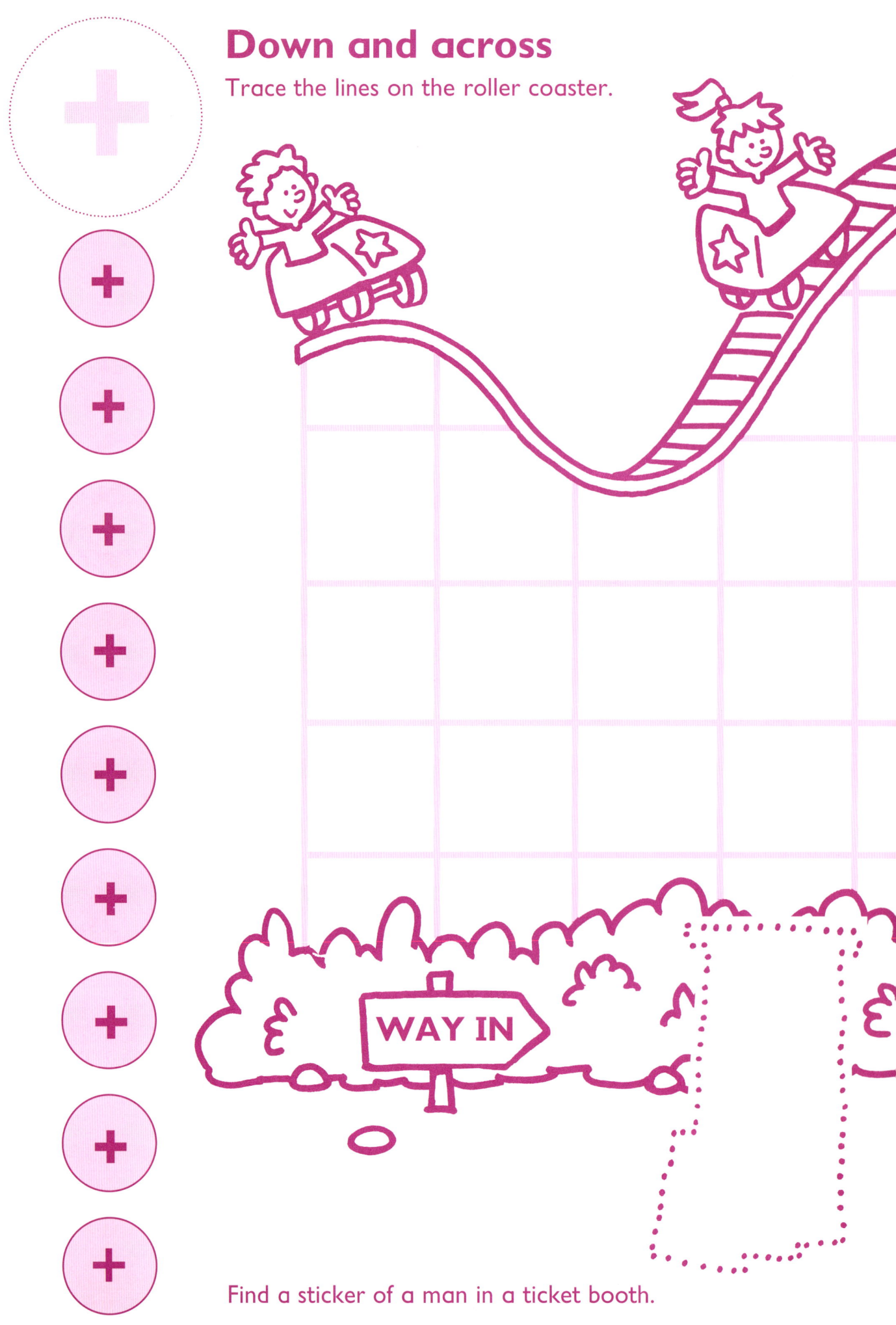

WAY IN

Find a sticker of a man in a ticket booth.

Well done! Put your reward sticker here.

Zigzags

Zigzag lines go up and down, up and down.
Draw a zigzag line in the air.

Trace the lines to draw sharp teeth on the big dinosaur.
Now draw spikes on the little dinosaur's back.

Here comes thunder!
Find a zigzag lightning sticker for the stormy sky.

Well done! Put your reward sticker here.

Wavy lines

Trace the lines to draw big waves in the sea.
Draw wavy lines in the sand.

Well done, now find a sticker of a bucket.

Well done! Put your reward sticker here.

Circles

Trace the lines to draw lots of circles.
Which are easier to trace – big circles or small ones?

Find a sticker of a big round ball.

Here are some more circles for you to trace.

Do you know which letters use a circle shape?

Well done! Put your reward sticker here.

Straight letters

Can you stand straight and tall like the letter l?
All these letters have straight backs.

l i t f k

Can you write each letter in the air? Use your finger like a pencil. Start from the top each time.

Now you are ready for some real writing!
Trace the lines to write the letters.

l is like a candy cane

i has a dot on the top

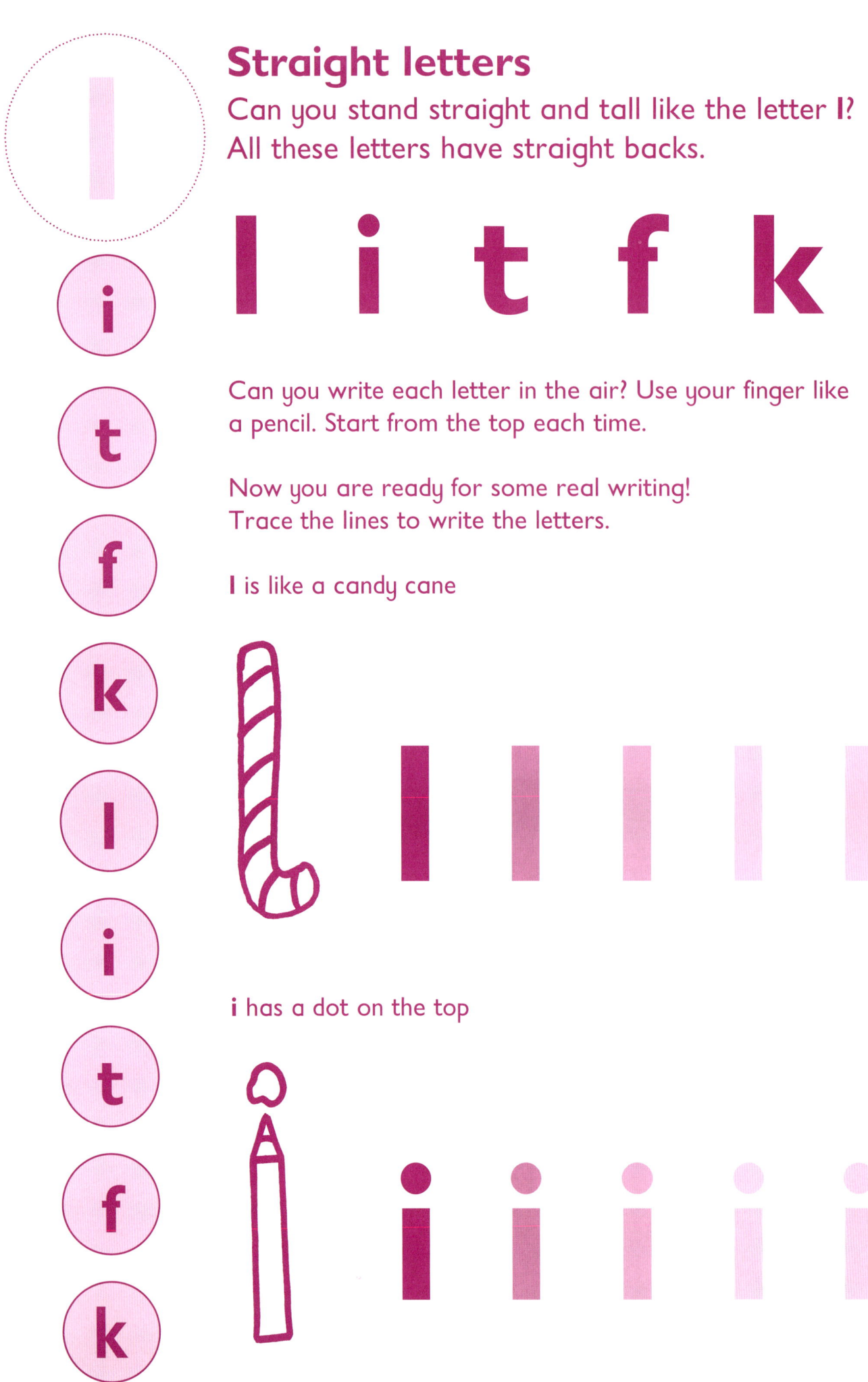

t curls up like an anchor

f is like a flower

k can kick like a footballer

Can you dance like a ballet dancer or march like a soldier, keeping your back very straight?

Find a sticker of a toy soldier.

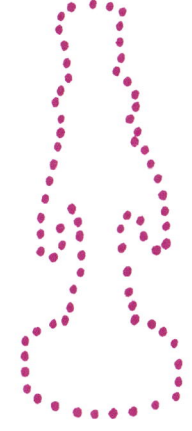

Well done! Put your reward sticker here.

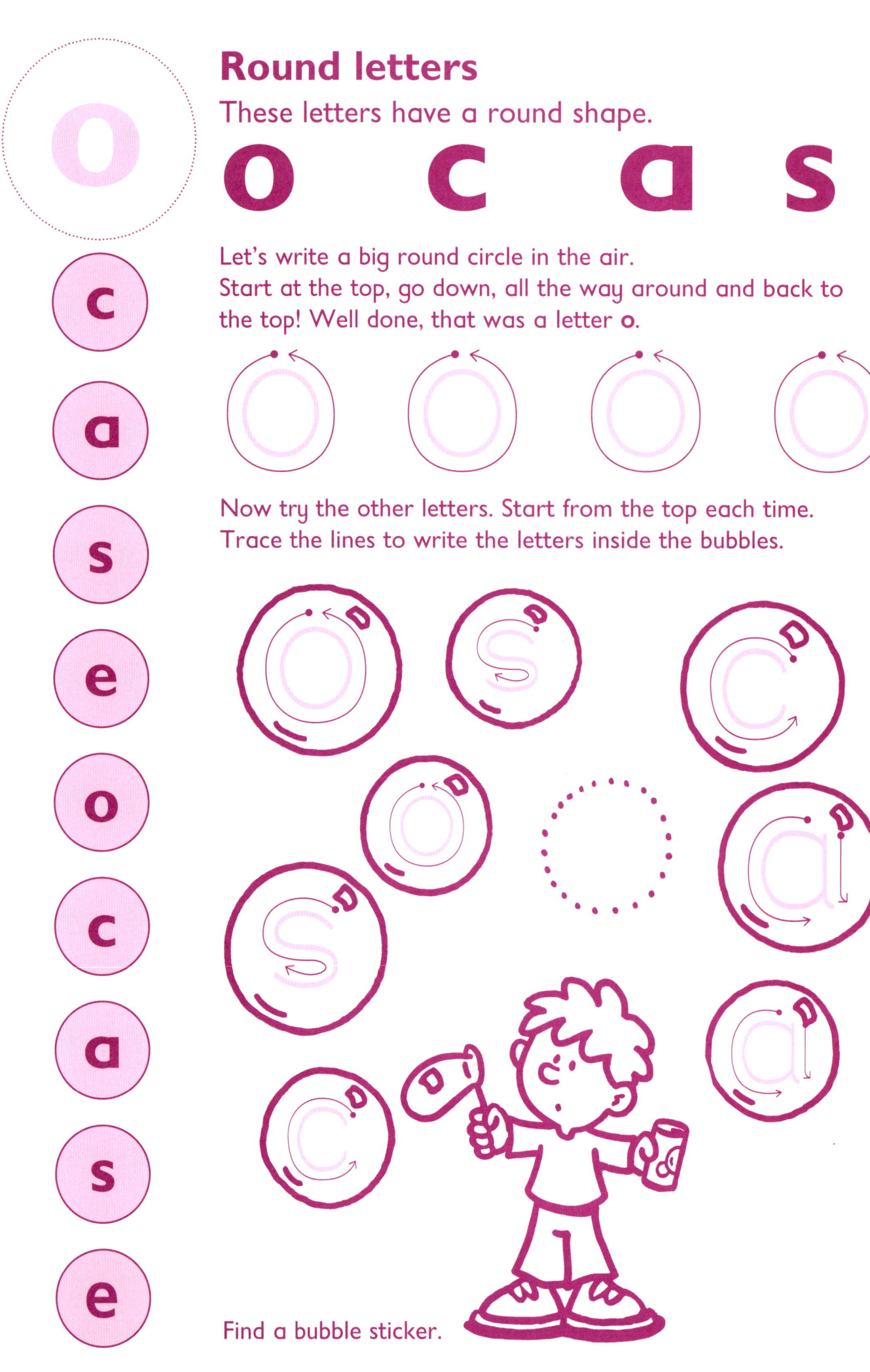

Round letters

These letters have a round shape.

o c a s

Let's write a big round circle in the air.
Start at the top, go down, all the way around and back to the top! Well done, that was a letter **o**.

Now try the other letters. Start from the top each time.
Trace the lines to write the letters inside the bubbles.

Find a bubble sticker.

e for egg

The letter **e** is round too, but we write it from the middle – from its tummy!
Can you write an **e** in the air?

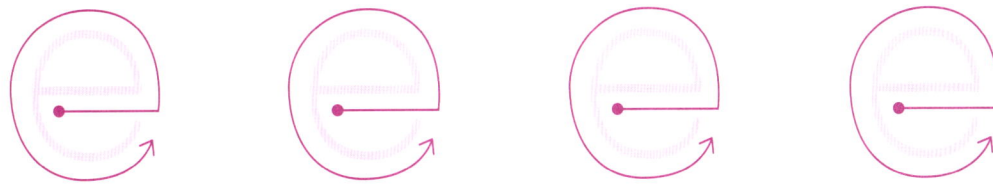

Now trace the lines to write **e** inside the eggs.

Do you have any round letters in your name?

Well done! Put your reward sticker here.

b and d

The letters **b** and **d** like **c**.
They always face **c** in the alphabet!

b and **d** have tall straight backs and round tummies!

We draw **b** from the top and **d** from the middle.
Draw them in the air.

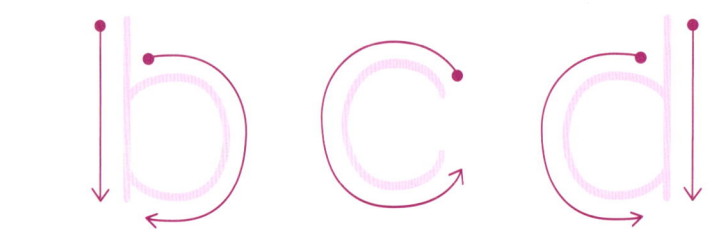

Trace the lines to write **b** and **d**.
Can you write the missing letters in these words?

_ e _

_ i r _

Best buddies

b and d are best buddies, but each likes different things.
b likes things that begin with b.
d likes things that begin with d.

Draw lines to the things they like.

b d

Letters with tails

These letters have curly tails.

j g y

Practise drawing them.
Start from the top of the letter. They all curl the same way.

j is like a sock

j j j j

g is like a monkey

g g g

y is like a yacht

y y y

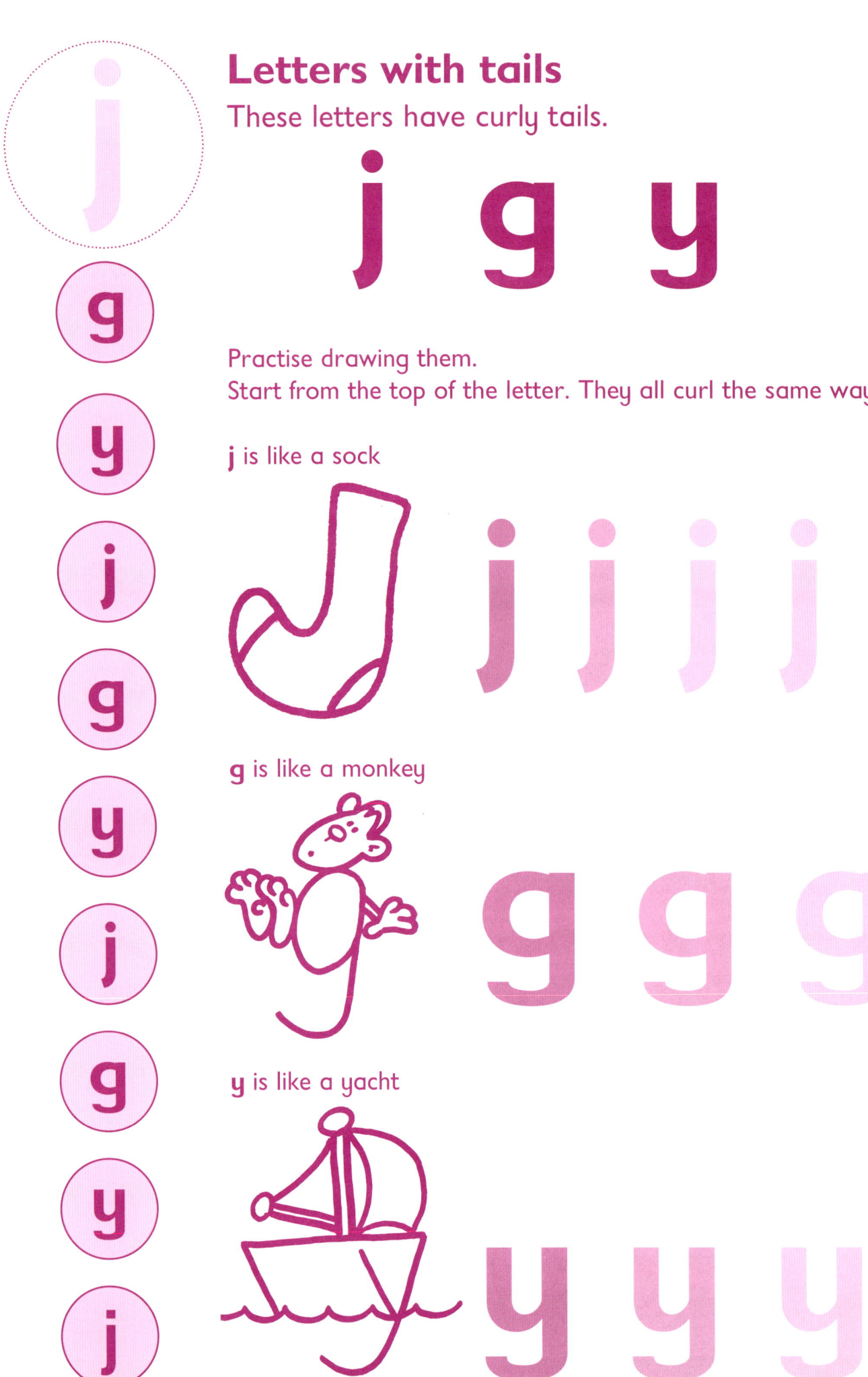

j g y

Trace the letters on the washing line.

j g y j y j j g y

Can you write the letters on the washing line?
Their heads go above the line.

_____

_____

Find a sticker of a cat.

Well done! Put your reward sticker here.

p and q

The letters **p** and **q** face each other in the alphabet. One of them has a pointy tail. Which one is it? Draw both letters in the air.

p q

Now trace the lines to write the letters in the sea. Make sure they keep their heads above the water!

Find a sticker of a baby penguin.

Pat-a-cake

Write the missing **p**'s in this rhyme.

Pat a cake, __at a cake, baker's man.
Bake me a cake, as fast as you can.
Pat it and __rick it and mark it with __,
and __ut it in the oven for baby and me!

Find a sticker of a cake.

Write **q** on one of the cakes. That cake is for the queen.
Now write the first letter of your name on another cake.
That one is for you!

Well done! Put your reward sticker here.

Straight lines and curves

These letters have straight lines and curves.

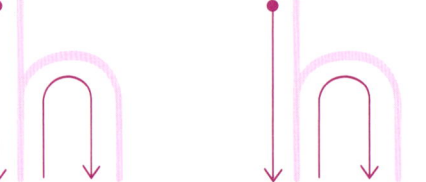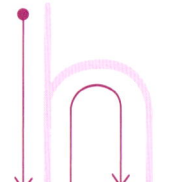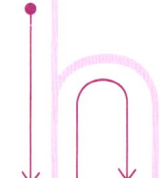

They are all the same height, except one.
Which letter is taller than the others?

Can you write these letters in the air? Now trace them.

Do **m** and **n** remind you of little round hills?

When you write **m** you go...
down the hill and up the hill, down the hill and up the hill,
and down the hill again!

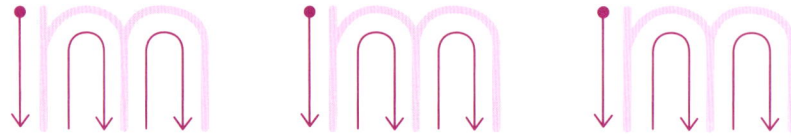

Find a sticker of Jack and Jill.
They are climbing up the
letter **m**.

Upside down u

Does the letter **u** look upside down to you?

What letter does **u** make if you turn it upside down?

Write **u** in the air with your finger. Then trace the lines to write the letters.

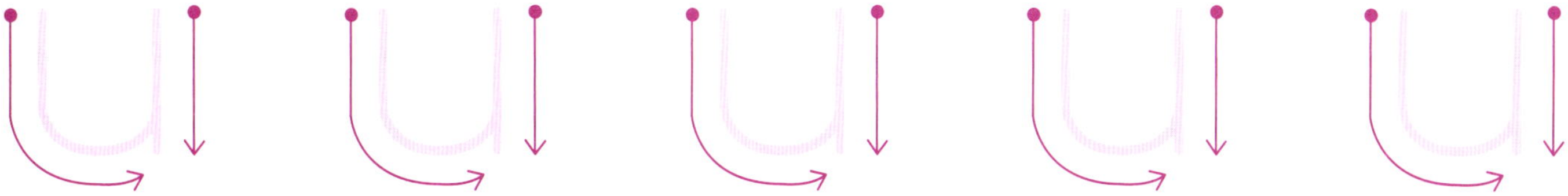

Can you write the missing **u** in this sentence?

Una has an _mbrella!

Find the sticker of Una.

Well done! Put your reward sticker here.

Different directions

These letters have straight lines that go in different directions.

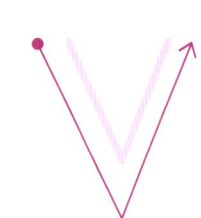
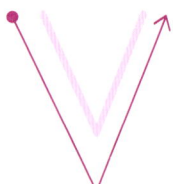
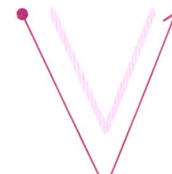

v is like a candlestick

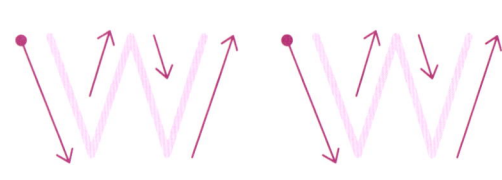

w is like this table

x is like the thread on a button

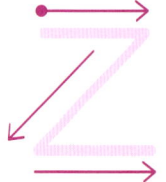
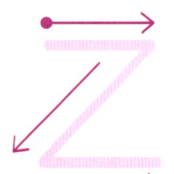
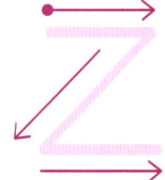

z is like a slithering snake

Find a sticker of a shirt.

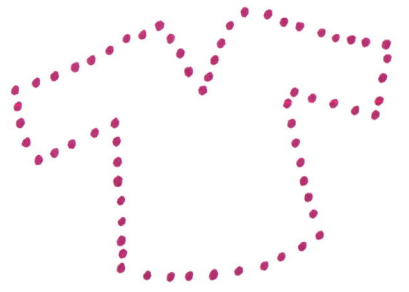

Trace the letters to finish the words.

vest

bow

box

zip

Find a sticker of a bow.
Can you write the missing letters in this sentence?

A bo_ with a bo_.

Well done! Put your reward sticker here.

Copy cats

Trace the letters. Then find a matching letter and draw a line to connect them.

a

b

c

d

e

f

g

h

i

j

s n t

n x e

f

f

e

s x

t

Find a sticker of a cat that looks the same as this one.
Have found the copycat?

Amazing alphabet

Starting at the letter **a**, trace the letters of the alphabet in order, and find your way through the maze.

start

finish

Well done! Put your reward sticker here.

Number names

Now you know how to write all the letters!
Let's put some letters together to make words.

Write the missing letters to finish the number names.

ten	10
_ine	9
eight	8
_even	7
si_	6
_ive	5
four	4
thre_	3
_wo	2
one	1

10 9 8 7 6 5 4 3 2 1

Find a sticker of a planet.

Colour names

Here are some more important names.

Write the missing letters to finish the colour names.
Colour in this picture using as many of the colours as you can.

_ellow
_range
_ed
_urple
_lue
_reen

Well done! Put your reward sticker here.

This is me!

One very important name belongs to you!
What's your name?

Draw a picture of yourself in the picture frame.
Write your name underneath it in your best writing.

About me

Write words in the spaces.

I am _____ years old.
My favourite word is _____ .
My best friend is _____ .

Which of these things do you like to do?
Write **y** for yes, or **n** for no, in the boxes.

Well done! Put your reward sticker here.

Twinkle, twinkle, beautiful star

Trace the lines to draw a big star.
Colour the star using the letter code.

y = yellow   b = blue
r = red   o = orange
g = green   p = purple

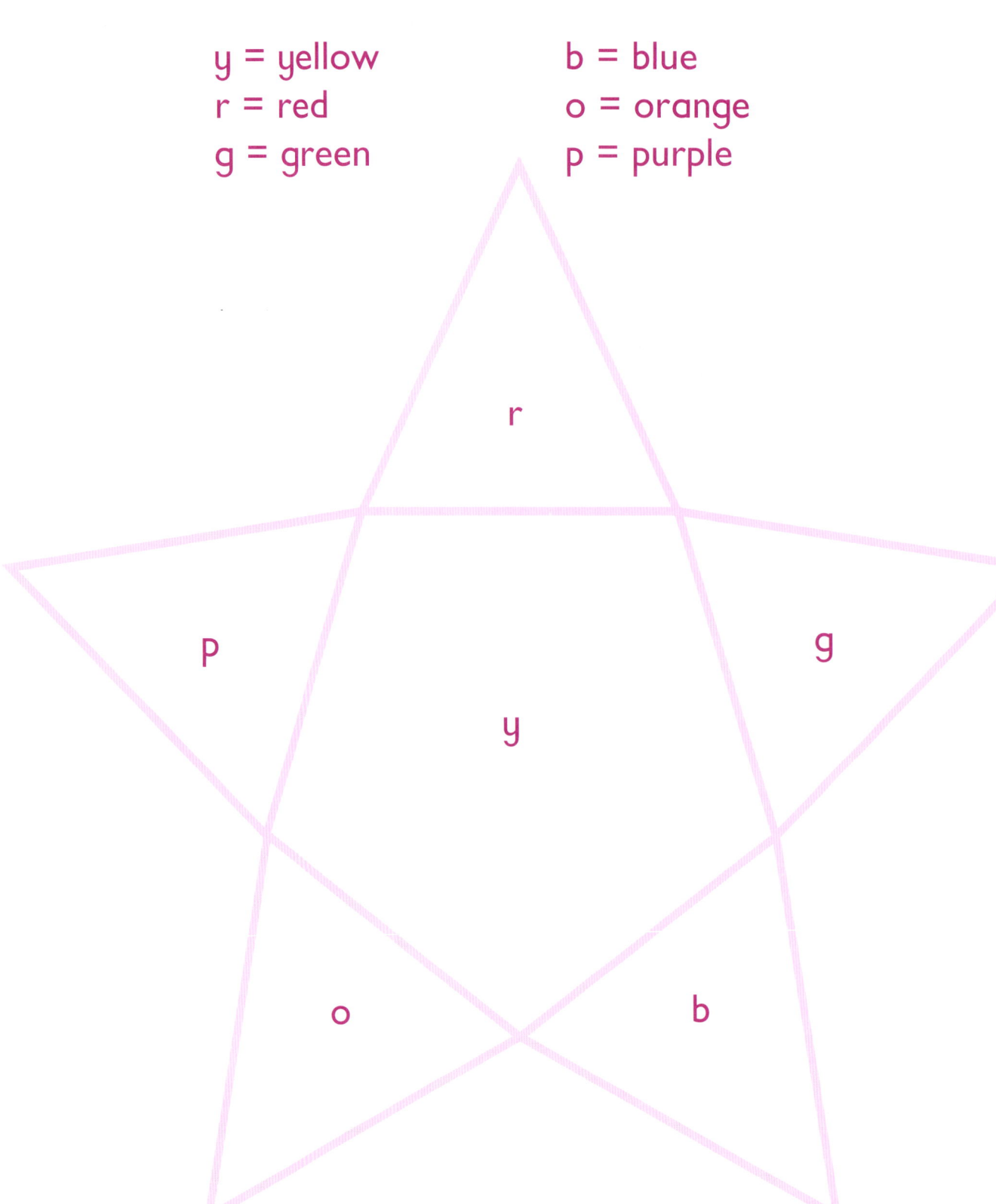

Well done. It really is a beautiful star now
and you are a star for finishing this book